THE EFFECTIVE THERAPIST'S BRAIN DUMP

CREATED BY:

Deirdre F. Haynes, Ed.S, LPCS

DEDICATION

This book is dedicated to all the hardworking mental health therapists in the world that seek to create more efficient and effective systems in their business!

© 2018 Deirdre F. Haynes.
All rights reserved worldwide.

This publication is protected under the US Copyright Act of 1976 and all other applicable international, federal, state, and local laws. No part of this work may be reproduced, distributed, or transmitted in any form or by any means, without the prior written permission of the author.

In the case of brief quotations embodied in critical reviews and certain other noncommercial uses permitted by copyright laws, excerpts from the text may be used. It is requested in these instances to include credit to the author and if possible, a link to www.theblindspotbiz.com.

For permission requests, please contact the author directly at:
support@theblindspotbiz.com

Dear Therapist,

I created *The Effective Therapist's Brain Dump* because I understand. Keeping up with the "people work" and the "paperwork" is often a major, overwhelming undertaking that is never fully completed. Many of us, spend our nights and weekends working at home or in our offices on client treatment plans, notes, billing, or some other aspect of the therapeutic process in an effort to simply keep up!

If you are like me, you always have at least five balls in the air that you are constantly juggling. Even though we are superheroes, it can become overwhelming at times. Sometimes, getting our thoughts together enough to figure out where to start digging into all the "stuff" we have to work on throughout the day is the hardest task of the day.

Never fear superhero! Help is on the way! I created *The Effective Therapist's Brain Dump* so that you will be able to take all of the rambling thoughts out of your head and get them onto paper so you can make sense of it all. Simultaneously freeing up brain matter so that you can be more present with your clients. Doesn't that sound great?

To get started, please check out the Legend on the next page to learn step-by-step how to use this system.

Before you go....

If you desire to learn more about how to use any of my To-Do Lists and other business-related tips and information, you can check out my YouTube channel (**Deirdre Haynes**).

Also, be sure to visit my website, www.theblindspotbiz.com, to get more information about my other productivity products and services. You can also sign up for my *VIP Email* list there as well so that you do not miss out on discounts and other exciting offers that I provide only for those that are on my email list.

Thank you so much for your purchase!

Deirdre

Graphic Organizer Pages

Sample Graphic Organizer

Directions: Use this section to create a graphic organizer that indicates your yearly or monthly goals. The key to the Brain Dump is to simply allow your thoughts to flow. Don't think too hard about them. Simply get them onto the paper. You can analyze and decipher what you wrote at a later time. So, let's begin….

*This is a simple example of one type of graphic organizer you can use to "map" out your yearly or monthly plans. You can continue to draw arrows and boxes which adds more layers and steps to the process. **The clearer it is to you the more likely you will get it done!**

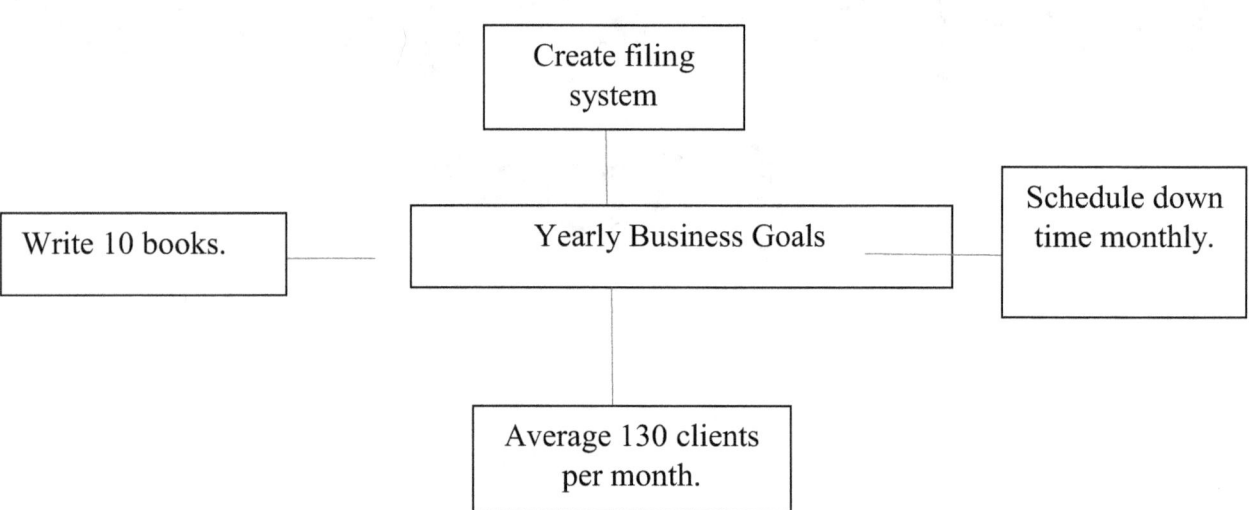

Graphic Organizer

Directions: Use this section to create a graphic organizer that indicates your yearly or monthly goals. The key to the Brain Dump is to simply allow your thoughts to flow. Don't think too hard about them. Simply get them onto the paper. You can analyze and decipher what you wrote at a later time. So, let's begin….

Graphic Organizer

Directions: Use this section to create a graphic organizer that indicates your yearly or monthly goals. The key to the Brain Dump is to simply allow your thoughts to flow. Don't think too hard about them. Simply get them onto the paper. You can analyze and decipher what you wrote at a later time. So, let's begin….

Graphic Organizer

Directions: Use this section to create a graphic organizer that indicates your yearly or monthly goals. The key to the Brain Dump is to simply allow your thoughts to flow. Don't think too hard about them. Simply get them onto the paper. You can analyze and decipher what you wrote at a later time. So, let's begin….

Graphic Organizer

Directions: Use this section to create a graphic organizer that indicates your yearly or monthly goals. The key to the Brain Dump is to simply allow your thoughts to flow. Don't think too hard about them. Simply get them onto the paper. You can analyze and decipher what you wrote at a later time. So, let's begin….

Graphic Organizer

Directions: Use this section to create a graphic organizer that indicates your yearly or monthly goals. The key to the Brain Dump is to simply allow your thoughts to flow. Don't think too hard about them. Simply get them onto the paper. You can analyze and decipher what you wrote at a later time. So, let's begin….

Graphic Organizer

Directions: Use this section to create a graphic organizer that indicates your yearly or monthly goals. The key to the Brain Dump is to simply allow your thoughts to flow. Don't think too hard about them. Simply get them onto the paper. You can analyze and decipher what you wrote at a later time. So, let's begin….

Graphic Organizer

Directions: Use this section to create a graphic organizer that indicates your yearly or monthly goals. The key to the Brain Dump is to simply allow your thoughts to flow. Don't think too hard about them. Simply get them onto the paper. You can analyze and decipher what you wrote at a later time. So, let's begin….

Graphic Organizer

Directions: Use this section to create a graphic organizer that indicates your yearly or monthly goals. The key to the Brain Dump is to simply allow your thoughts to flow. Don't think too hard about them. Simply get them onto the paper. You can analyze and decipher what you wrote at a later time. So, let's begin….

Graphic Organizer

Directions: Use this section to create a graphic organizer that indicates your yearly or monthly goals. The key to the Brain Dump is to simply allow your thoughts to flow. Don't think too hard about them. Simply get them onto the paper. You can analyze and decipher what you wrote at a later time. So, let's begin….

Graphic Organizer

Directions: Use this section to create a graphic organizer that indicates your yearly or monthly goals. The key to the Brain Dump is to simply allow your thoughts to flow. Don't think too hard about them. Simply get them onto the paper. You can analyze and decipher what you wrote at a later time. So, let's begin….

Graphic Organizer

Directions: Use this section to create a graphic organizer that indicates your yearly or monthly goals. The key to the Brain Dump is to simply allow your thoughts to flow. Don't think too hard about them. Simply get them onto the paper. You can analyze and decipher what you wrote at a later time. So, let's begin….

Graphic Organizer

Directions: Use this section to create a graphic organizer that indicates your yearly or monthly goals. The key to the Brain Dump is to simply allow your thoughts to flow. Don't think too hard about them. Simply get them onto the paper. You can analyze and decipher what you wrote at a later time. So, let's begin….

Graphic Organizer

Directions: Use this section to create a graphic organizer that indicates your yearly or monthly goals. The key to the Brain Dump is to simply allow your thoughts to flow. Don't think too hard about them. Simply get them onto the paper. You can analyze and decipher what you wrote at a later time. So, let's begin….

Graphic Organizer

Directions: Use this section to create a graphic organizer that indicates your yearly or monthly goals. The key to the Brain Dump is to simply allow your thoughts to flow. Don't think too hard about them. Simply get them onto the paper. You can analyze and decipher what you wrote at a later time. So, let's begin....

Graphic Organizer

Directions: Use this section to create a graphic organizer that indicates your yearly or monthly goals. The key to the Brain Dump is to simply allow your thoughts to flow. Don't think too hard about them. Simply get them onto the paper. You can analyze and decipher what you wrote at a later time. So, let's begin….

Graphic Organizer

Directions: Use this section to create a graphic organizer that indicates your yearly or monthly goals. The key to the Brain Dump is to simply allow your thoughts to flow. Don't think too hard about them. Simply get them onto the paper. You can analyze and decipher what you wrote at a later time. So, let's begin….

Graphic Organizer

Directions: Use this section to create a graphic organizer that indicates your yearly or monthly goals. The key to the Brain Dump is to simply allow your thoughts to flow. Don't think too hard about them. Simply get them onto the paper. You can analyze and decipher what you wrote at a later time. So, let's begin….

Graphic Organizer

Directions: Use this section to create a graphic organizer that indicates your yearly or monthly goals. The key to the Brain Dump is to simply allow your thoughts to flow. Don't think too hard about them. Simply get them onto the paper. You can analyze and decipher what you wrote at a later time. So, let's begin….

Graphic Organizer

Directions: Use this section to create a graphic organizer that indicates your yearly or monthly goals. The key to the Brain Dump is to simply allow your thoughts to flow. Don't think too hard about them. Simply get them onto the paper. You can analyze and decipher what you wrote at a later time. So, let's begin….

Graphic Organizer

Directions: Use this section to create a graphic organizer that indicates your yearly or monthly goals. The key to the Brain Dump is to simply allow your thoughts to flow. Don't think too hard about them. Simply get them onto the paper. You can analyze and decipher what you wrote at a later time. So, let's begin….

Graphic Organizer

Directions: Use this section to create a graphic organizer that indicates your yearly or monthly goals. The key to the Brain Dump is to simply allow your thoughts to flow. Don't think too hard about them. Simply get them onto the paper. You can analyze and decipher what you wrote at a later time. So, let's begin….

Graphic Organizer

Directions: Use this section to create a graphic organizer that indicates your yearly or monthly goals. The key to the Brain Dump is to simply allow your thoughts to flow. Don't think too hard about them. Simply get them onto the paper. You can analyze and decipher what you wrote at a later time. So, let's begin….

Graphic Organizer

Directions: Use this section to create a graphic organizer that indicates your yearly or monthly goals. The key to the Brain Dump is to simply allow your thoughts to flow. Don't think too hard about them. Simply get them onto the paper. You can analyze and decipher what you wrote at a later time. So, let's begin….

Graphic Organizer

Directions: Use this section to create a graphic organizer that indicates your yearly or monthly goals. The key to the Brain Dump is to simply allow your thoughts to flow. Don't think too hard about them. Simply get them onto the paper. You can analyze and decipher what you wrote at a later time. So, let's begin….

Monthly To-Do Lists

Here is how it works....

1. Write down the date that you plan to complete the task in the **DUE DATE** section.
2. Write down the abbreviated key word that stands for what the task is that you need to complete in the **KEY** category. ***A recommended Legend that you can use is below***. Feel free to personalize your Legend to fit your individual needs.

LEGEND

KEY	DESCRIPTION
B	BILLING
C	CLIENTS
D	DISABILITY PAPERWORK
E	EMAIL
I	INSURANCE (i.e. claims, credentialing, follow-up, form submission, etc.)
N	NOTES
C	CALLS
H	HOUSEKEEPING (i.e. filing, cleaning, check mail, check voicemail, etc.)
M	MEETING
T	TREATMENT PLANNING
W	WORKSHOP

3. Write down the actual task you plan to complete in the **TASK** section.
4. Put a check in the **DONE** box when you complete the task. I also recommend pulling an (arrow) in the box if you need to move it to next week.
5. That's it! You're officially a counseling rock star!

DUE DATE	KEY	MONTH: _____ TASK	DONE

DUE DATE	KEY	MONTH: _____	DONE
		TASK	

DUE DATE	KEY	MONTH: _____ TASK	DONE

DUE DATE	KEY	MONTH: _____	DONE

DUE DATE	KEY	MONTH: _____	DONE
		TASK	

DUE DATE	KEY	MONTH: _____ TASK	DONE

DUE DATE	KEY	MONTH: _____	DONE
		TASK	

DUE DATE	KEY	MONTH: _____	DONE
		TASK	

DUE DATE	KEY	MONTH: _____	DONE
		TASK	

DUE DATE	KEY	MONTH: _____	DONE
		TASK	

DUE DATE	KEY	MONTH: _____	DONE
		TASK	

		MONTH: _____	
DUE DATE	KEY	TASK	DONE

		MONTH: _____	
DUE DATE	**KEY**	**TASK**	**DONE**

DUE DATE	KEY	MONTH: _____ TASK	DONE

DUE DATE	KEY	MONTH: _____	DONE
		TASK	

MONTH:			
DUE DATE	**KEY**	**TASK**	**DONE**

DUE DATE	KEY	MONTH: _____ TASK	DONE

DUE DATE	KEY	MONTH: _____	DONE
		TASK	

DUE DATE	KEY	MONTH: _____ TASK	DONE

DUE DATE	KEY	MONTH: _____	DONE
		TASK	

		MONTH: _____	
DUE DATE	KEY	TASK	DONE

DUE DATE	KEY	MONTH: _____	DONE
		TASK	

DUE DATE	KEY	MONTH: _____ TASK	DONE

DUE DATE	KEY	MONTH: _____	DONE
		TASK	

DUE DATE	KEY	MONTH: _____	DONE
		TASK	

Other Books By Deirdre F. Haynes

Nonfiction Books about Relationships

The Quick and Dirty Guide to Infidelity
The Cheatsheet: Who Are You REALLY dating?

Nonfiction Books about Business/Writing

The Quick and Dirty Guide to Starting Your Business
The Quick and Dirty Guide to the Effective Writer's Mindset
Blindspots: Everything You Didn't Know You Needed To Know About Starting Your Private Practice

Productivity and Organization Workbooks

The Big Book of Communications
The Effective Therapist's Weekly To-Do List
The Effective Therapist's Daily To-Do List
The Effective Therapist's Brain Dump

Therapeutic Workbooks and Journals

The Vault: General Edition
The Vault: Therapist's Edition
The Vault: Group Therapy Edition
The Vault: Anxiety Edition
The Vault: Depression Edition
The Vault: Journal For Men
The Vault: Journal For Women
The Vault: Gratitude Edition

LET'S STAY IN CONTACT!

Deirdre F. Haynes, Ed.S, LPCS, NCC, DCC is a psychotherapist in Columbia, SC. She owns Deirdre Haynes Counseling Services and an online self-help store, The Blindspot Biz.

To purchase any of her books, e-books and audible books on Amazon, please visit:
http://bit.ly/deirdrehaynesbooks

To Subscribe to her YouTube channel: www.bit.ly/DHaynesYoutubechannel

Deirdre Haynes Counseling Services:
Appointments (SC only): www.dhaynestherapy.com
www.facebook.com/dhaynestherapy
www.instagram.com/dhaynestherapy
www.twitter.com/dhaynestherapy

The Blindspot Biz: Online Self-Help Store
(Products/Courses/Blog/Email List)
www.theblindspotbiz.com
www.facebook.com/theblindspotbiz
www.instagram.com/theblindspotbiz

Mailing Address:
Deirdre Haynes
P. O. Box 290902
Columbia, SC 29229

www.ingramcontent.com/pod-product-compliance
Lightning Source LLC
Chambersburg PA
CBHW062340220526
45469CB00008B/2781